tulsa non-poems

DR. WALTER MOORE

Columbus, Ohio www.empbooks.com

First Edition:10 19 33 34 6 11 1973
ISBN: 979-8-88596-189-9
LOC: 2024944131
Design, Layout, and Edits: Ezhno Martín
Cover Photo : Mural on the side of 510 W. Chapel St, Columbus, OH

CONTENTS:

(p.p.s. / **xo**).

Over my head, I see the bronze butterfly,
Asleep on the black trunk,
Blowing like a leaf in green shadow.
Down the ravine behind the empty house,

The cowbells follow one another
Into the distances of the afternoon.
To my right,
In a field of sunlight between two pines,
The droppings of last year's horses
Blaze up into golden stones.
I lean back as the evening darkens and comes on.
A chicken hawk floats over, looking for home.

I have wasted my life.

— James Wright

Hi, How Are You?

— Daniel Johnston

Inhale . . .

. . .*Exhale . . .*

. . . *Inhale . . .*

. . . *Ex--*

Godammit so it goes
ladies and gentlemen and
all else . . .

. . . last fall up in Oregon . . . after the pandemic
lockdown that contributed to a handful of
personal batshit mental collapses . . . after
teaching on sinister Zoom for hundreds of
mindnumbing online hours and grading
thousands of undergraduate papers and talking
into the void and cracking my brain on a
computer screen while battling poorly considered
self-medications . . . after halting my university
teaching career of two decades . . . after my
mother in Texas had a bad stroke . . . after a
bunch of other family drama and crises . . . after
going through an intensely messy and quick and
painful divorce of a twelve-year relationship and
marriage . . . after a slow few years' build-up of
said relationship's demise . . . and throw in a few
close friends going through divorces and mental
breakdowns too . . .

after dropping out of a graduate program I
actually liked . . . after my ex-wife lost her mind
. . . after I relinquished the house and dog and
new car and the majority of the bank account
based on ethical principle . . . after all of it . . .
in a frenzy I put select belongings in my 2009
Toyota Corolla, a humble compact that has
been to Mexico and Canada and about 40 U.S.
states (*a car with 180,000 + miles: knock on
something*),and drove south and east through

the American desert for the Lonestar winter
holidays to help my mother recover, to be there
for my family as best I could, to connect with
old friends as best I could, and to help myself
recover with added sunshine . . .

.   . . . *Exhale.*

      In other words . . .
      I had just come off a hellish quarter . . .
      A season of discontent . . .
      I was free but I was broken . . .
      And dammit . . .

I do miss my dog.

         ("Hi, how are you, Lloyd?")
So it goes.

      I thought I was going to live in Austin,
a city I loved living in during my twenties in
the early part of the twenty-first century, but
after a nervous breakdown around New Years,
and after a bunch of other mishaps that piled
present colloquial trauma on top of residual
trauma(s) of violence and uprootedness, after
numerous panic attacks and successfully deep
frying my already cooked nervous system and
even getting diagnosed with godforsaken P.T.S.D.
during those Texas winter holidays, sunshine
included, I decided that the hyper-traffic and
freneticism of this New Austin in 2022/2023—a
college town on steroids with strong perpetual
shots of Big Tech and Reality Show Dreams—
was just too much; the city, which I regardless
still love (e.g. the live music, breakfast tacos,

my dear old friends) wasn't where I was at (and I'll admit maybe Thomas Wolfe was more right than I had originally surmised after all); it wasn't what I needed, so after doing what I could for my mother, after meditating for 200 hours on a farm 6.5 miles east of Austin, after doing long barefoot runs anywhere and taking cold plunges in an apartment complex pool to aid recovery, after a schizophrenic meth addict showed up to said farm with a gun to kill a good friend of mine, again after a number of those hideous panic attacks and feeling like I was going to die, after ringing in my ears and hallucinations for days on the floor of a trailer in Rockport, Texas, too terrified to face the world, after not sleeping for a year and a half leading up to this demise of marriage, et al, after crying to the point of dust and Buddha, I decided to make some phone calls to people in other places to see if there was a more appropriate place to go.

Despite it all the Oregon woods and the sheer striking natural beauty of the Pacific Northwest did/does beckon, and I admit I still might return there one day, but I did not want to get too far away from my Texas family and friends even though I had come to realize that Austin is not the answer either. At least not for me. (Plus, I was tired of driving.) I considered a move to New Orleans, Houston of course is another labyrinthine behemoth even though I know some very good people there too, I've never understood Dallas, San Antonio was too close, Oklahoma City has never quite melded just right, and I even pondered Albuquerque.

Yet Tulsa.

And Tulsa.

*So: Tulsa.

Tulsa, Oklahoma?

During January of 2023, as I recovered with those barefoot runs and cold plunges and endless prayers, off-the-cuff confessions to Catholic priests and meditations with Buddhist monks, I continued to have phone conversations with a friend of mine in Tulsa, and the more we talked about the place the more I knew this city could make sense: I know some good people here, and I've always had a great time when I've visited; it's relatively affordable, easy to get around, has nice people, is a medium size (400,000 in the city proper), and enough pound-for-pound cultural amenities for creatives (*SEE: Leon Russell, Church Studio, Mercury Lounge, Cain's Ballroom, S.E. Hinton, Larry Clark, Shades of Brown, Circle Cinema, The Center of the Universe, the Tam Bao Buddhist Temple, et al.)

I don't know how long I'll be here, but it is more than good for now — "three months or thirty years in Tulsa" has been my recent mantra. Regardless, it is an underrated locale, and I will be forever thankful for this city.

(*Gratuitous Aside: And I'll also just say I haven't watched television in over a year. I barely use the

internet other than to check email and weather,
and I still have a flip phone, choosing to keep my
computer(s) and telephone separate. No, I'm not
a Luddite. But I do prefer physical reality. For
example, just to name one example: online dating
seems dehumanizing. I'd rather not treat another
human [myself included] as a utilitarian item on
a menu that can be callously scrolled through and
dismissed like reheated roast beef and/or like leftover
late-night Tiramisu. I'm not saying I'll never use
these technologies. I just don't feel a compelling
need to use them currently. Yes, I am admittedly
of the opinion that we do live in a technocracy
that has turned too many people into half-robots.
Autonomous, independent thinking is on the decline,
and I've decided to play my small part in slowing that
disintegration down. But whateverthefuck.)

Call me a romantic?

Fine, I am a romantic.

None of this has been easy of course,
but I've learned many valuable lessons during
this season, and I am grateful. Grateful for the
people in my life. And grateful for so much of
the world, good music included. So much of
what drives this collection of non-poems is
the music I was listening to and inspired by
these last few months. Among other notables, I
could never have been able to heal without the
music, especially my recent Tulsa Sound music
exposure, and I am, yes, again, grateful. And
I'll say that I've titled this collection Non-Poems
because that's where my mind-space mainly
has been the last few months: confused yet clear
and in complete sentences; sincere, earnest,

straightforward, grieving yet hopeful, not to mention on-the ground pedestrian, anxious, quiet, and occasionally conversational.

Pure non-poetic *ThankyouGod*, really-*reality*.

(*Another Aside: I've never liked writing poems that friends and family couldn't understand anyhow. And I'll say that I learned this approach mainly from Albert Huffstickler, patron saint of Austin and about the best poet to come out of that city that I can think of. Rest in peace, Albert.)
If my first book of poems was my "punk rock album" then this second one is the "break-up album," but, regardless of labels, writing this most recent collection has been cathartic. It genuinely helped me get through a difficult period.

In this collection, as a kind of soft tour-guide list for other wayward travelers, I've also italicized some of the places of this city I've frequented and hold in high regard (*e.g. Thelma's Peach*).

*So:

Long live Tulsa Time & Space, a proper portal . . . and Tulsa, thank you from the depths of my broken though healing heart. I truly mean that.

Many blessings.

Dr. Walter Moore. March/May/August 2023

There is no Oregon or Oklahoma or you or me or black or white or red or blue—only right and wrong: the truth ***and everything else. This has been the most challenging and intensely emotional, worst/ best year of my/your life, but I/you (and we) are better off. We are*** lucky.

Thanks for reading.

And thanks for the screaming light. Cheers to all of it and all of you,
Walt

(July 2023)

p.s. The 30 albums that helped me the most during this season (*in no particular order):

1. *Another Side of Bob Dylan*
2. *Horses*, Patti Smith
3. *The Nashville Sound*, Jason Isbell
4. *Demon Drivin' Blues Man*, Howlin' Wolf
5. *The New OK*, Drive-By Truckers
6. *Transcendental Blues*, Steve Earle
7. *I Know What Love Isn't*, Jens Lekman
8. *The Original Soundtrack of the Royal Tenenbaums*
9. *Better Man*, Lance Roark
10. *Weight of a Trigger*, Lost Dog Street Band
11. *I Be Trying*, Cedric Burnside
12. *Songs of Faith and Devotion*, Depeche Mode
13. *Glory*, Lost Dog Street Band
14. *Eternally Even*, Jim James
15. *Yoshimi Battles the Pink Robots*, The Flaming Lips
16. *Inside Taj Mahal*, Paul Horn
17. *Alone & Acoustic*, Buddy Guy and Junior Wells
18. *Copperhead Road*, Steve Earle

*<u>ZERO</u>

XO (burn after writing)

"It's all in the art. You get no credit for living."

—David Shields, *Reality Hunger*

"Outside a Cloud" or
"Travis – Paris, Texas" or
"I Just Got a Divorce" or ...

[1] FOR SHARON MOORE

. . . after pomegranate and dancing acoustics

. . . . . . spent last night in Joshua Tree

in . . .

. . . the Mojave and from above . . .

. . . the town's lights of
personal and commercial buildings
looked like fireflies, if fireflies had no
way to fly.

The fireflies walk to the
corner markets and hope
not to drive till Sunday
afternoon.

I knew I would start my car
before then.

And now sleeping in that same car in Marfa,
3:57 a.m. in an RV park, outside a
cloud and can't find the key to get in.

Patron Silver high, the stars have sky
and Monday looms already. Where are
the medicine men? Never mind I drove
900 miles today through two deserts
and broken-hearted strip malls.

The oyster is a world, and my Japanese
compact has never seen so many clothes.

The emperor had a closet.

Divorced

now, from a woman and a place and
all of it, but on common ground, a
familiar hallelujah and down to one
pack, lights not ultra, my actual
preference. Time to sleep upright,
pray for alright and a second half
of a life that doubles down as better
than. So goes that man—a dream and
a hopscotch, a vision of water not in
a bottle, nor people you pay for. All
of it a happenstance for some kind of
solution. Call it salvation. Call it all of
us.

xo

—*10/31/22, Marfa, Texas*

[2] GRAND PRIZE

—*for James Moore*

"To know that what is impenetrable to us really
exists, manifesting itself as the highest wisdom
and the most radiant beauty . . . this knowledge,
this feeling is at the center of true religious men."
—Albert Einstein

And sitting here at the Grand Prize
bar off the Boulevard in between
Montrose and Rice Village close
to Hermann Park and sometimes
Shakespeare under moonlight,

I think of God as a verb
rather than noun, as energy
rather than entity—

and the poet Rilke thought of
God as direction rather than
object, and that this direction is
towards the best and highest I
and we can conceive,

that we feel and
exhibit this energy
without thinking;

it has become as natural
as drinking water—

and alone here on the
balcony, a second-floor
patio of the Grand Prize,
that feeling you get on a
Wednesday night in Houston
in the middle

of December, a Cramps song
playing on the jukebox, the
bartender a kind person, and
you go outside to 65 degrees
and a blessing

that your childhood city

still has soul, a soul, and

that maybe you are free,

truly free, for the first time

in your life,

and that the pure gaps are
in between traffic, air and
invisibility among cars,

and your brother whom you love
so dearly as you prolong a hug
around his broad shoulders,

he carried the weight for you
at times so much too,

and in this moment
you do feel the energy
of the bayou air,

the glorious stillness of the
Rothko Chapel earlier, before
putting your quarters down
and going inside and playing
pool and thanking everybody

with your own dollars
in the jukebox.

You play Jason Isbell.

Sometimes being home
is to feel God too—

to feel the details of
our universal lives,

to fulfill the details of
your earlier promises,

the ones you made
to your family.

—*12/14/22, Houston, Texas*

[3] SITTING ON THE GROUND AT FRANCISCO SERNA'S FARM SIX-AND-A-HALF MILES EAST OF AUSTIN, TEXAS

—for Lawrence Ferlinghetti

Christ climbed down from his bare tree this year
and took it mindful at the RV park, helped fix the
septic tank, fed stray dogs on the property, made
soup for strangers who were only strangers
before soup.

Christ climbed down from his bare tree this year
and went to the dumpster behind the Hole in the
Wall, turned plastics into vegetables and Lone
Star into forgiveness.

Christ climbed down from his bare tree this year
and walked backwards through Jack in the Box
turning patty melts into pineapples and daisies
for our minds' eyes—

Christ climbed down from his bare tree this
year and vanquished all baby computers along
with the uprooted trees of electricity and tinsel,
he made disappear a man in a red suit with a
fake white beard and type 2 diabetes—took the
mayonnaise out of the salad along with all of
the ammunition, gun barrels now used to clank
music.

Christ climbed down from his bare tree this year
to walk naked through the church parking lots;
he blocked the door at Best Buy with photographs
of the desert, not to mention miracles.

Christ climbed down from his bare tree this year
and told us that his birthday came in July and
that he died on Labor Day.

Christ climbed down from his bare tree this year
and went into the womb of an American senator
whom we haven't heard from since.

Christ climbed down from his bare tree this year
and walked into the middle of the highway and
is still walking the wrong way down the middle
of the highway and the Austin police department
have been called about it but they say they
approve, could use the help during a drunken
holiday season filled with raised levels of per
capita violence, the stress is too much, and Christ
still walks down the middle of I-35. He says he'll
go back on top the tree after everybody dances in
the river and realizes.

$-12/20/22$, Austin, Texas

[4] CLASS GRADUATION SPEECH, EDMOND NORTH HIGH SCHOOL, EDMOND, OKLAHOMA, 1996

It's June, the sun is out in Oklahoma, and
there are 365 of us here. In a couple decades,
a few decades, more than a dozen of us will be
dead, maybe another dozen or so in prison.

About half of us divorced. No billionaires, three millionaires, 22 of us will be homeless. Some homeowners, many kids, the majority will feel dissatisfied with their jobs, about 150 of you will cheat on your spouses, 320 will be addicted to something. Many Christians, a good amount will come out of the closet, a few even tomorrow a day after graduation. A handful will change their identities. Some of us will move out of the state, a few out of the country. All of us will die one day. There will be love and heartbreak and sadness and joy—loss, grief, new beginnings and second chances. Forgiveness, grace, betrayal, confusion, redemption. Wonderment. And later tonight, I'll see most of you at the afterparty in the field in the middle of nowhere. $5 per car. There will be one keg, and we'll run out of beer in the first fifteen minutes, then stand around talking about what we plan on doing for the rest of our lives.

—12/24/22, Rockport, Texas

[4.5] 21st-CENTURY USA

—for Patterson Hood

There are no cafes in Paris,

nor liquor stores,
only fast food gas stations,

a few body shops.

No bohemias, no fresh bread

or cheeses or walks along the Seine,
rather obesity and a crying baby
in the next motel room.
Three construction workers
drink large cans of Keystone beer
in front of their door.
The baby keeps crying.
Our Eiffel Tower
is a Dairy Queen.
Cultural pandemic filled
with ADHD and anxiety meds,
Botax and spray tans,
an American strip mall.

Here in Paris the BBQ comes
wrapped in plastic, and
we fight about identities,
share the same opulent
garbage yet yell about opposing
red and blue trashcans.
Here in Paris there are
no trains, only trucks
filled with crying babies and
musical lyrics written for
middle school children—and people
working hard for shrinking pay;
buying them prescription pills
and maxing them credit cards
via pocket computers.

I refuse to turn the television on
in this motel room in Paris.
Here in Paris the people are dying,
streetlights filled with fear and
waste along the highway.
Tulsa is not the answer nor

Houston or Austin, neither Oklahoma
or Texas—not NYC or LA or Kansas
City or Miami. Portland, no,
Providence,
no. Paris is not the answer.
The movie *Paris, Texas*
never gets to Paris.
Next stop: Athens.
And then Palestine,
Texas.

I hear there's a Whataburger
and a gun shop
instead of genocide
or enlightenment.
When, Paris, will you
seal the green emeralds
and patch up
the gashes of
our broken dreams?

—*11/25/23, Paris, Texas*

[5] REDUCE THE INTENSITY

"I defecate and nourish. There is nothing more to it."
                                        —Henry Miller

After nervous breakdown freakout,
and still feeling the anxious PTSD
residue here in the Antidote
Coffee Shop (wearing earplugs and
headphones, trying to hide the world),

in the Houston Heights, I am
trying to take it easy and

reduce my stress: I am terrified
at moments. Terrified of moving
forward, moving in general,
getting a job, making money,
starting my life over, being . . .

In Houston now but heading
to Tulsa next week, or so goes
the plan, and I am terrified. I'm
trying to be hopeful, excited
even, but I have a lot of anxiety.
Therapist told me today to try to
have "fun."

(Remember fun?) and maybe
laugh, so I'm trying to read this
Nick Hornby book, *Songbook*
(reading on the "light" side) and
drink a little coffee and take it
easy, but I feel the anxiety.
Hornby's book does make
me think of music that is
important, so I'll try to write
a non-poem about that:

Steve Earle always made me
think of black coffee on the
countertop of a diner, good music
playing in the background. And
Patterson Hood reminds me of a
bonfire and then looking up and
seeing fireworks that are not
related yet fitting.

Jason Isbell smooth top shelf
mescal sipped slowly.

Nirvana never reached
enlightenment, and MTV died.

Digital did kill the Television Star.

Never mind the Bollocks. Georgia
on my mind and morning glory,
Big Star killed many rock stars.

I remember so many times . . . dancing to

The Beastie Boys in an empty
swimming pool in Brooklyn, Ghostland
Observatory, Patti Smith at

CBGB, Pavement in Central Park, Moby
Grape's Jerry Miller (the greatest guitar player
I've ever seen with my own eyes)
playing to nine people at a bar
in Springfield, Oregon;
the Vandals and Pearl Jam in a
bicycling arena in San Sebastian,
Spain, Phish at the Gorge, Kenny

Rogers at the Astrodome, Sage
Francis in a R.I. warehouse,
shaking hands with Bob Dylan
at Willie Nelson picnics and
dancing with Willie's sister—

Spoon on a roof deck, sleeping
in The Killers penthouse in the
Lower East Side, Beck at a dive
bar in Austin, Modest Mouse in
Louisville with 18 people on a
Wednesday night,

Wayne Coyne's kitchen, and Wolf
Parade in a small vintage clothing
store while they blew the lid off.

We shared a keg.

So many nights and concerts and
rendezvouses, the heartbreak nostalgia along
with pleasant memories, music has been the
background and soundtrack of my life,

always there pushing me through and beyond the
nervous frenzy. Even now.

—1/28/23, Houston, Texas

[6] MOVING TO TULSA

To be alone is to rumble in
the dark corridor of a familiar
neighbor's hallway— only to
realize your neighbor is you and
his mind your mind. The cave in
your chest has bats, your body a
cliff of steep ledge. The bats hit
rock and if you look closely you
will see the cliff does shake, and
your neighbor's voice echoes
beyond the ruins.

*

In the Rothko Chapel
the people were obelisks
moved by canvases.

Grey inside matched
the grey out. The sky as
waiting room for trees.

This town used to be a
swamp, but you wouldn't
know it. The cars move here
like an electric carnival.

*

At Agora Coffee Shop off
Westheimer, I think of Rene
Magritte and raincoats.
The Menil Museum is free
to get in, and in one display
there's African pottery and
tools belonging to ancient
kitchens, which is all to say it's
time to live again.

*

Now at my good old friend Tony's house in
the Heights. Tony is a successful person, a
technology executive in petroleum. And a good
man.

After I finish this cigarette, I'm about to take a
shower in his mother-in-law suite.

Tony is treating me to dinner
tonight, but I'll give him twenty
dollars, which is all a Buddhist poet
can afford. Tony is hoping to depart
his industry soon, maybe travel the

world on a boat or perhaps buy a bar.
I think at dinner I'll tell him about
the time I did ayahuasca in the
Oregon woods with some shamans,
and how our dreams are the same:

Poetry and boats of moving light.

We both need to live our lives.

—2/1/23, Houston, Texas

*ONE

—I dedicate this
book of poems to
the friends and
family members
who helped me get
through this past
year. You know who
you are. I could not
have done this

alone.

TULSA NON-POEMS

"No you ain't baby. That cat is a prince . . . He is
royalty in exile. You ain't never gonna look like
that."

—S.E. Hinton, Rumble Fish

On a t-shirt at the Mercury Lounge:

Too broke for
Austin.
Too stoned for
Nashville.

*

[7] BROKEN CYCLE

At *Arnie's Bar*
I imagine my
grandfathers, whom
I've never met, walking
past each other after
spotting someone else. My
grandmothers, whom I
did meet, waiting at home
longing for someone to tell
them they genuinely love
them.

I just got a divorce,
and in a booth alone

in the back of this
place, perpetuating my
family dynasty

yet looking
for no one.

*

Now at the Mercury Lounge
writing with a pen I found that
says *University of Wyoming*
down the side of it.

The celloist on stage
finishes her last
song, and '90s hip
hop follows out of
speakers.

A shot and a beer
is five dollars,

which does remind me
of the nineties.

My cousins are here
talking to strangers.

It's a Thursday and
I think I'll take the
weekend to hibernate

far away from family,
not in Wyoming

but in a garage apartment
in Tulsa.

— 2/15/23

[8] S.E. HINTON GOT IT RIGHT

At the *She Brews Coffee House* in
the Kendall-Whittier neighborhood,
corner of Lewis and Admiral, I see
the "Stay Gold" marquee next to the
Circle Cinema.

Sunny Saturday morning
and the *Farmer's Market*
across the street has
mainly breads and meats,
vegetables and patrons
waiting for spring.

Whitty Books isn't open
yet, I sit in this coffee shop
created by women— there are
seventeen women here
(four behind the counter), five
men including me and one
baby bouncing on a knee while
sucking his mother's thumb. The
energy of women has always
carried me through difficult
patches, this period no different.

I've come to Tulsa to find
inner peace, the beautiful
strong women in my life
cheering me forward.

I am not alone though
there's black coffee by
myself.

In about an hour I'll go see a noon matinee across
the street, *Everything Everywhere All At Once*,
then maybe go to *Thelma's* down
the way or perhaps to the
The Outsiders House,
now a museum

co-owned by Danny Boy O'Connor
of House of Pain lore.

Stay gold indeed.

Diane Lane was incredible in
that movie as Cherry Valence,
and I'm sure the women of this
coffee shop would approve,
a strong young woman
surrounded by and not giving up
on broken men,

boys really,

with redemptive qualities.

—2/18/23

[9] HAVEN'T ACHIEVED ENLIGHTENMENT YET

After doing a mixed work-out
(soccer ball and basketball drills,
some distance running, push-ups,

sprints) at the *Gathering Place*
where multiple generations
commune for morning cardio,

I swing by *Shades of Brown* (33rd and
Peoria) for a large Columbian coffee. I
do enjoy the art on the walls. This is not
a poem, as I feel I have nothing at the
moment. Nothing left to give, but I am
working on that. Or maybe this is a poem
about nothingness.

—2/19/23

[10] LONG LIVE CEDRIC BURNSIDE

At *Another Round on Brookside*,
I do think about my contexts:
How long can I stay in one place?
Five years seems pushing it. My
conditioning and familiarity,
vagabond tendencies no doubt.
Going

to get a shot and beer, play a
game of pool and then walk
back to *Casa Shores* to eat fried
chicken with the children.

This has been a pleasant
day. Have a few months to
decide if I will be returning
to Eugene in September
(maybe June? July?
August?) which gives me at
least some biding to settle

into Tulsa Time and see how
it goes. Have fun? I will try
my best.

You can still smoke in bars in
Tulsa, which I can't believe.
Now playing pool, drinking a
shot of Evan Williams and a
Lone Star

and smoking a cigarette
inside a bar. What kind of 20th
Century portal am I in?

Right now I do think of my
good friend Hank Anderson.
Hank from Cushing, Oklahoma,
just down the highway. Hank
who died in a car wreck in
the middle of a sunny day
between Denver and Durango.
Hank and I loved to play pool
together, and if I don't miss
him now, two poseurs with
sensitivities who just might
punch a bully in the mouth if
need be.

At least we would have done
that more than a decade
ago. I play pool, sometimes
poorly and sometimes well,
depending on the liquor
consumption, and anyway
here are my thoughts. Read
if you feel like it. If you

don't feel like it, there are
quarters on the table and the
next round is on me.

You might find yourself

in a non-poem too— if
that means anything
to you.

But if it doesn't, I am
pleased to meet you.

Your assumptions are
probably right:

I've lived everywhere in this
country, been everywhere,
seen most—talked to many,
my own ethnographic
research. If you look at my
contexts: born in Singapore
and lived in Indonesia; 40
countries, 47 states, but it's
more than that too. The real
truth is that I am curious—
about people and the world
and this country and myself
and I can't seem to stop.

But I'll just say that I love
this country and the people
in it even though I don't agree
with everybody or all of it. My
love is there, even amid the
disagreements. Because to
disagree is to be human,

and my quarters will
always be on the table,
for anybody, and the next
round is on me, and if
there's a jukebox then even
better. I'll play whatever
you prefer.

Cedric Burnside
or Cyndi Lauper,
doesn't matter,
they're both
great.

I just hope we all can
dance together when
the moon shows up and
we have taken off our glasses.

—2/20/23

[11] SHADES OF BROWN

After completing my morning routine
at the Gathering Place, walking
along the path to the Corolla,
I saw a bald eagle perched high
on the branch of an oak tree
next to the river.

Purely regal and grey, a beak
for timeless memory. I
sat on a bench and looked up to
him for a long time, existing,
lit a cigarette, and he strong-
eyed a mating call to another

eagle across the way on an
adjacent tree before she flew
towards the river, the Tulsa
Electricity Company
sign in the distance.

And he sat there,
I sat there, feeling the energy
of the moment. A reminder
of being alive and I was
thankful. A few people gathered
to honor him too and we quietly
acknowledged our lovely fortune.

Eventually he disappeared, the
small crowd dispersed, and I
walked back along the path to
the Corolla.

At Shades of Brown now
the older gentlemen at the
coffee bar counter talk
glowingly about Bruce
Springsteen who is playing
at the BOK Center tonight:

"High energy. Even in his seventies." "No matter
who you are you cannot deny that he is a powerful
singer."

"Six bucks for a ticket in
the upper row."

"The millennials don't
 know him."

"The young people just like
the commercial stuff made
on the computer.
Made only for a party. No
substance."

"Wonder if good music
will ever come back."

"It probably will."

These older men talk about the band
Kansas and how they struggled for
years and finally broke through
because they were talented musicians,
not just people messing around with
computers—and how computers have
taken the soul out of music.

And tonight Bruce Springsteen.

On Thursday Bad Brains,
NYC/DC punk royalty, will play
at *The Shrine*. I do aspire to
see live music these days at
least once a week.

Amid the gentlemen, I met a sleep specialist
here at Shades of Brown named Monty who told
me about tennis options at *LaFortune Park*, so
hopefully I can get involved with that soon too.

A metal band from Pittsburgh is
playing at the *Whittier Bar* tonight,
says Clay, a local musician who
works behind the counter.

If I choose, I think I'll see
H.R. of Bad Brains instead
of The Boss.

There's an energy to Tulsa—a musical energy,
a creative source, and a hospitable and kind
and decent humanity.

It has been a transcendent morning,
and I think about that bald eagle and
do thank him for all of it— along with
The Boss and H.R., and those
gentlemen too.

It is Tuesday and

Bad Brains and the rest of our
lives in an oak tree, along the
river, at a coffee shop, and at
The Shrine, and
I do agree that the good music

will
indeed come
back again.

—2/20/23

[12] BIG FISH

At the Mercury Lounge again. Tuesday at 3:30
p.m., grey overcast day and I do think about
these poems. Are these poems? The answer
doesn't matter; poems, prose, prose-poems,
fiction, non-fiction, 'tween, mind to fingers

to words on pages; images, rhythms, stories,
musings, otherwise. The human mind
as documented: written, edited, rearranged,
yes, but documented and put down as
artifact, as a memento and physical object
for retrieval, at least memory, a vault. An
impermanent vault but a vault. A temporary

capsule, and I can live with that.

Yes, I'm at the Mercury Lounge again.

They play good music here, live and
otherwise. The rain is coming. Tomorrow
rain. Big Fish,

working the door, seems like a good
man, a tattooed punk rock white
beard bear

saint,
kind

and fierce (as needed), and I
appreciate his presence.

How did I get to Tulsa?

Long story involving losing my mind during a
pandemic lockdown, a divorce, near death, a
mother's stroke, a drive through the American
desert and a few tortured months in Texas, and
many prayers, and hopes for a second or third or
fourth chance. Eleventh chance? My repetitions
bother me, but I am trying.

Since October I've been grasping this country
again, and
myself, and the people I love, a lifelong grasp,
but/and

I am holding on.

Thank God for friends. And the phone
calls of family, not to mention the one
Buddhist temple here in town

(the *Tam Bao Buddhist Temple*
on 16933 East 21st Street

past 161st Street, founded in 1993 and Vietnamese
but "practices teachings of the Buddha in a
nonsectarian format"),

and meditations after hot showers and mantras
such as

This too, you motherfucker, shall pass.

Found out my Aunt Patsy died today. Patsy,
89, Houstonian, who has traveled the world.
Married to my Uncle Buddy who died a few years
back. I remember Patsy smiling at a wedding
in Copenhagen. She liked cruises and smoking
cigarettes while tanning by pools in
The Woodlands. That's what I remember. And her
daughter Diane, my cousin in Houston, is a sweet
person. So this non-poem is for the both
of them. For Diane. And Patsy:

May she have the peace she sought.

That's all anyone wants: Peace. The
price of gold, which is why the New Age
gurus have vacation homes.

I don't know. Poor Patsy. Poor all of us.
Family members dying or having bad luck
back there in Texas, which is part of the
reason I am in Tulsa. Hoping to have
better individual luck.

They say we can create our own good
luck, which I do hope is true.

Maybe I'll ask Big Fish about this later.

But yes: Death and bad luck and broken
dreams. Sometimes I look at photographs
of family members and friends when they
were children and think about them as
adults. I see these children and wonder if
they know what they are about to get into.

I look at photographs of myself as
a child and do wonder: *Boy*, do you
know that you'll be broken and
heartbroken writing a non-poem
on the front patio of the Mercury
Lounge on a Tuesday grey overcast
afternoon, listening to garage rock,
$5 shot and beer, reeling about
how the fuck any or all of it
happened?

What would you tell that kid?

Probably just to pay more attention, and never
smoke cigarettes. And go to therapy and just
know that your life will be a cliché country
song: Women and whiskey will do you in
repeatedly, but really you'll just do yourself in
time and time again. Just stop and think about
what the hell you are doing; and try not to
dwell on the past, and maybe stop writing
every once in a while. Maybe take up
woodworking instead. At least you'll have
chairs to sit on, artifacts that can't be
consumed on the internet.

None of it matters I guess.
Big Fish was once a child too.

And these cigarettes and cheap liquor
will kill me yet. At least I'm single, or
despite that I am single,

at least for a little
while here:

In Tulsa.

I guess that's a country song
too.

And graffiti is probably detritus.
But detritus with some truth in it,
as indicated by the writings on the
walls of the Mercury Lounge men's
bathroom.

And I did ask Big Fish about
creating your own luck:

He said only if
that's something you truly can believe
in your heart and that you need to
want it.

"Walt, you need to want it completely,"

he said.

— 2/21/23

[13] COLLAGES

The mind is not reality, we know this. Yet neither
is reality *reality*. Descartes wasn't quite right. We
don't think because we are. We are because we
don't think. We are not mind but rather no-mind,
or at least no-mind is closer to our truth. And call
truth reality.

Across the street is *Dalesandro's*, a perfectly
thriving Italian restaurant occupying one half
of a building. On the other half of the building
is the aftermath of a beloved local BBQ place
that recently scorched to the ground; the
charred rotted roofless remains of that previous
establishment: Italia shares a space with The
Apocalypse. Which one is reality: The neo-fantasy
or the memory? The truth is somewhere within
the dividing wall of the stark contrast, where the
windows of the BBQ place used to be.

I like the Swingin' Utters punk rock music
they are playing at the Mercury Lounge on a
Wednesday afternoon. It reminds me of that stark

contrast too. As the sun comes out beyond the graffiti, and the *HIPPIES PARK IN BACK* sign is large and on the front of the bar. It's true: I am lost in Tulsa. But I have nowhere to go anyway.

The Mercury Lounge is a special place, for any American city—because it serves as Ground Zero for just about every Tulsa musician. A kind of Red Dirt CBGB, yet it's 2023. And I've been here almost two weeks. The Mercury Lounge plays live music every night of the week. Every musician when I've mentioned the place has said some version of this to me: "Don't tell people about the Mercury Lounge." So I guess I won't tell anyone, unless you count this non-poem.

The truth is I'm not doing well.

I can't shake my memories no matter how many $5 shot & beer specials.

Maybe I'll get another job tomorrow.
Maybe I'll get drunk again.
Maybe I'll do neither.
Play tennis, edit this non-poem,
then go eat at Dalesandro's.

Possible titles for this one:

"I Do Yoga in the Morning so I Can Feel like a Human at Night."

"I Am Terribly Sober Around Drunk People."

Do we define ourselves by objects?
Or what's written about us on paper?

This is a lost year.

On t-shirts at the Mercury Lounge:

> *MAMAS DON'T LET YOUR*
> *COWBOYS GROW UP*
> *TO BE RACISTS*
> *THROWBACK PUNKS*
> *AND DAYTIME DRUNKS*

And the best one (*the one I will buy before leaving Tulsa):

> *TOO BROKE FOR*
> *AUSTIN*
> *TOO STONED FOR*
> *NASHVILLE*

When you are in Tulsa, go to the Mercury Lounge. But don't tell anyone I told you.

I just met a woman, an artist named Tangerine who goes by Tang, who has offered me a room for rent at her house (11th and Darlington/$675 a month + utilities).

I do feel like a dog who was raised for dogfighting. In mid-fight, the dog decides to walk away. He knows fighting is not right, but he also feels lost if he is not fighting. It is what he was conditioned to do.

Life is a collage.
Yours and mine. A collage.

No one knows what is going on inside
the mind or body of anyone else.

David Shields says that collage is a
demonstration of the many becoming one,
with the one never fully resolved because
of the many that continue to impinge
upon it.

We are collages.
All of us

at the Mercury Lounge.

—2/22/23

[14] STILL A.M.

I didn't go to church or a temple this morning;
I ate cereal and drank coffee and smoked
cigarettes (three cups and five weeds thus far
and on my fourth cup and probably will smoke a
sixth after writing this), took a shower and came
back here. I will most likely drink bourbon and
cheap beer later instead of meditating, praying,
exercising, cleansing, or doing something good
for the world.
But notice I've said "probably." I have the rest of
the day to turn my life around.

And in the news: Public defenders are having
panic attacks, Putin won't agree to a nuclear

arms treaty, Zelensky would like more sanctions, education vouchers are being voted on, the First Lady went to Africa, Brittney Griner is returning to the WNBA, R Kelly got 20 years, a fairly well-known actor died, sex trafficking is on the rise, there's a poetry reading at the University of Tulsa on Tuesday night, and the First Friday Art Crawl will occur downtown towards the end of the week.

The *Tulsa World*.

It's nearly afternoon.

—2/26/23

[15] BLOSS

. . . on stage tonight, his voice sounds like a soul if a soul were teaching other souls how to not to get hurt. His voice—and I don't think he knows what to do with it. Write this name down: Justin Bloss. He is 34 and has been doing it for 18 years and is one of the best singer-songwriters in Tulsa and probably the state of Oklahoma. Do help this guy make a living . . .

—3/5/23

[16] HALL OF FAME

Old man shuffles by on the Mercury front patio after smoking a cigarette in a booth. Back of his black polyester jacket says:

Shuffleboard Missouri State Champion
2000
Hall of Fame

White tennis shoes, khakis, grey
hair parted neatly, walking hunched
into the parking lot to his car before
Happy Hour.

The sun just broke through the clouds
after two days of overcast, and I think
about death, rebirth, when that
winning puck hangs on the back edge
of the table and all has been realized.

—3/9/2023

[17] THE BRAIN TO THE HEART

Wish I could yawp through a horn, not a
non-poem, but here it is: You have fallen
into disrepair, a thorn bush and your arm
tries to reach a key in the soil below you,
cross-bleeding and grasping for anything,
bats unruly, blind, reeling towards the
white flag. . .

I'd say black flag but Henry Rollins
is paranoid in his bunker too—so
white flag white flag white flag white
flag . . .

and tall orders for the screaming light.

—3/14/23

[18] NATIVE LAND

The old man with the Hall of Fame Shuffleboard
jacket makes his way for Happy Hour. The sun has
been out most of the day and the young couple on
the front patio are quarreling about television.
A young man in a wheelchair tells stories to
enraptured ladies. Sunglasses and cigarettes, a
woman with a black jean jacket with a rainbow
on the back of it, middle of the rainbow the word
LUCIFER—she is wearing a red t-shirt cut above
the navel; the band Big Star plays out speakers
and half of the building across the street still
burned out. A man in white cowboy hat with a
blue feather sticking out of it sits next to the Hall
of Famer. The kid who is going to Basic Training
in two weeks stands drunk at the bar with two
beers. The "You Are On Native Land" sign behind
the bar close to the Oklahoma flag and American
flag, free pork tacos by the stage, and the Circle
Jerks now play out of speakers. A young guy
named Danno Simpson from Ft. Collins, Colorado,
will play his guitar tonight. I think about Tulsa,
the garage apartment, my family, ex-wife, how I
got here— none of it makes sense and none of it
adds up. The terror persists but the hope is still
there. Where will I be a year from now? A month?
Will I recognize? The Hall of Famer finishes his
beer and shuffles out the door. I am afraid of
loneliness. But I do know that if he can do it then
I should do it, still a puncher's chance of that Hall
of Fame. And later in the night Danno will say
on stage, "Heaven is a Dallas whore," and though
he is a very talented young musician, he will be
wrong. Heaven is the sound of a guitarist, maybe
a banjo player, with the soul of God who plays for
sun.

—3/15/23

[19] RUBICON

Edge of ocean,
Whitmanic dividing
line of land and water,

and I think about the Oregon
Coast, Yachats in particular,
as I sit on this velvet couch
in Shades of Brown. A long
line waits for the coffee
counter, a line that includes
a 6'8" center

(Nate Clover III) for the
Oral Roberts basketball team.
Spanish music plays out the stereo,

I stare at a painting of Frankenstein
and a painting of William Burroughs,
which I would like to buy,

the Spanish music plays on as the line
continues with the buzz of grinders.
Walt Whitman was right: there is

something powerful about
where the land meets the
ocean, where people wait in
line for liquid and stop

looking at screens, then realize
the world as we know it is about to
change, that everything ahead of us

will involve floating.

—3/24/23

[20] STILL 5 DOLLARS FOR A SHOT AND BEER

The pain knobs turned up
high in that one's brain—

he sits corner of bar writing a
lifeline that makes its way into
this non-poem's life. He plays later
in the night with his band, says
before one song:

"This song is about a bold-faced
lie from someone you love."

He is sad and he is talented, and,
indeed, he is royalty in exile;
however, you do wonder if all
the sadness is necessary, if we
should let Hank Williams or the
'90s sleep.

For not everybody loves playing
music in Tulsa and that is okay
too,

but I will mention that
royalty in exile does not exist
only in this town.

—4/4/23

[21] MONASTERY ROAD

At the *Osage Forest of Peace*, I
listen to the birds talk and sing

and know that God speaks
through them too.

The wind fills the gaps in the trees as
do the silences between the bird calls.

This Oklahoma
landscape off
Monastery Road
overlooking the hills
offers respite from the
many voices backing
urban entropy.

I sit on a rock of a bluff
trying to reduce the fear
that the wind or the birds
won't hear my calls either,
that the spaces I create

won't fall away to our
common unity.

—4/5/23, *Osage Forest*

[22] RED DIRT SUNSET - AFTERNOON GRATITUDE

—*for Pam & Richard*

At the Wilshire Club,
thinking about the
kindness of strangers.

Some people do break my

heart in good ways, and I will
hold on to that.

The Wilshire looks the same: two
pool tables, Madonna then Gotye
then The SteelDrivers play,

same old regulars chainsmoking
at the bar talking about Easter,
arthritis and eternity.

Time to get going now while
hope is alive in me that the
world could open up again

for daylight's offerings— because
when the sun hits your eyes after
stepping through the backdoors

of the windowless Wilshire, you'd
better be ready to say a prayer for
all of it.

—4/8/23, Oklahoma City

[23] SAINT FRANCIS

What happened? they asked.

In the empty chapel of the St. Francis Hospital
(61st and Yale) I did thank God.
Thankful my mother's illness wasn't
worse and other current blessings. It has
been a hell of a year,

but I am still here, living with hope
and addictions and the gritty dotted
lines and ditches alongside.

The mountains in the desert were signs.
That river in Texas a sign.

As was the dog with diabetes and the two
other dogs playing in the dirt.

She has been in the hospital for a week
now, poked and radiated, hundreds of
thousands of dollars for scans, poorly
written reports, bad food and
kindness—

only to release her into an
unhealthy world that does not have
her better interests in mind. Yet I
pray, and I still

hope that one day we
can get it right, that we
can realize—

our endless generations' fallacies as the
products of minds' design and recent
spirits starved amid synthetic lights and
re-circulated air.

What happened? you ask.

She did what you told her.

—4/21/23

[24] SPRING

Today is my brother James's 50th birthday,

and Depeche Mode plays out of speakers,
which seems fitting—

Brandon Clark about to play,
a Tulsa hero and good person.

Afternoon sunshine on this
patio, an older wise man talks to
a receptive young musician.

Now Danzig's "Mother" plays.
Danzig, and all your music video

glory, people here do love
you, too.

Cheers to my brother James.

He is sort of like Danzig,
might punch you then buy
you a drink and laugh about
it afterwards, show grace.

And yes Danzig still plays— and
the live music is about to begin.

Brandon Clark on acoustic,
the rest of our lives— and,
sure, his rendition of
"Drunken Poet's Dream" is
truer than you realize in
this moment.

The songs afterwards are penance.

Penance for the dreams unrealized
before the rain tomorrow, before
the sun after that, before you
understand in this moment that
we will laugh about the winter
while holding flowers, smelling
graves

and tops of heads
of newborn
babies.

—4/23/23

[25] FAMILIAR FEELING

In the *Quick Trip* parking lot near
LaFortune Park, rainy Wednesday
limbo, I think about the reasons for
losses alongside Steve Earle out car
speakers—

familial terror
revisitations and all the
text messages
in the world will not stop
that.

Why is that/what is *that?*
The return of thinking about
and potentially loving
something or someone more
than myself. The return of
vulnerability, sacrifice and
the images of a beautiful

though impermanent world.

The return of what got me here
in the first place.

—4/26/23

[26] CRISS-CROSS TO NEON

At the Gathering Place on a
grey Thursday afternoon,
no one else sits in front of the pond, and in my
solitude the water moves right-to-left, which
contradicts left-to-right thinking

and reminds me to go another way. The
large orange coy fish criss-cross as nearly
neon, paying no attention to the perimetric
urban conditioning of Red Dirt development.

The chairs of the pond's beaches bare waiting
for eternity
to sit back again or at least an eagle or smaller
bird to perch notice.

The willows lean in to the moss at attention
with kindly regularity,

all a premonition for evening's mysteries,
all a snapshot of weekday serenity.

— 4/27/23

[27] GENE KELLY AND ERIC CLAPTON NEVER DID THIS. MAYBE BOB WILLS OR WOODY GUTHRIE DID. I'M SURE LEON RUSSELL GANDERED.

Perched on a rock on *Turkey Mountain* while
meditating, below I see a mountain biker fall
and hit a rock. He is fine, gets up and walks his
bike slowly up the incline.
Strange toys these bicycles and helmets.

Barefoot with my shirt off, I like the happy dogs
who walk the path.

No one seems to see me sitting up here,
which I prefer.

I'm not a voyeur, I'd rather be alone,
but this birds' purview
is interesting—better than internet-television
or even Circle Cinema.

Nothing more positive than a forest, in
Oklahoma or Oregon or anywhere.
Not even the river. The ocean is close
but tells too many horror stories. The
forest has mystery too, and its magic is
more forgiving.

My soundtrack the birds, my
cinematographer the sun & sky,
rubes in helmets: extras; naked
dogs leads in romantic comedies.

I can still hear the car noise beyond,
and no stopping that rush though I'd

like to not hear it every once in a while.

Maybe next week I'll head to Cherokee land,
ask questions of no one.
Only of myself and the shadows dancing like stars
to the sun's direction and The Great Mystery's
chords.

   — 5/1/23

[28] PLEASE LEAVE A MESSAGE

After getting out of the Corolla, a Cadillac
disguised as a donkey,

I walk into the middle of the drained-out
Arkansas River off the *Riverside Park* path, sit
on a rock, and take in the glorious wasteland
that could be a set on a George Lucas movie, or
at least Mel Gibson's megachurch. Striations of
flat and jagged rocks dominate small brown pools
of water (ripples of one pond perfect) and sewage,
small birds on rocks tentative of offerings:
freeway bridges, modest industrial plant and
generic apartment buildings
as backdrop,

yet gazing downward I take in the
post-Apocalyptic groundswell of
humanity's misstep; drinking San
Salvadoran coffee out of a used
cup from Braum's— with Portland
cowboy boots,
Indiana tattoos, Portuguese sunglasses and
Singapore birth, Texas

cheerleaders, soul in transition—
smoking Oklahoma Native American reservation-
field tobacco sold to me by a friendly Iranian man,
and looking West:
Could be in Eugene in 30 hours driving-time
yet Tulsa holds me at least through May:
"Three months or 30 years in Tulsa"
has been my recent mantra though it's
almost been three months and I might
not have 30 years. The usual
distractions recently: women and
whiskey and music and fantasies, but
what I truly long for is that pure spirit
trip,
like that time in the Oregon woods
or that other time on a Balinese
beach, another moment in New
Zealand and/or The American
Desert. Yes, the West does wink at
me, call me (sometimes leaving a
message) with loaded temptation
and confusion. And sitting here
the last few months with my
mostly urban meditations
I do wonder if I'll pick up the phone next
time, or even call back and tell her about all
of it.

        —5/3/23

[29] WOODY GUTHRIE

Local lore's there's a
naked ninja that strikes
downtown, takes off his

clothes and does karate,
presenting more than an
open hand. They've seen
him by the *Blue Dome
District* and the *Guthrie
Green*. I'm sure Woody
Guthrie would approve:
His machine killed fascists
while the naked ninja kills
local investment. I hope I
see him in person one day,
and can buy him a drink
or a sock

for property value, his
and theirs.

—5/4/23

[30] - P.S.

 *Graffiti written on the walls of the Mercury men's bathroom:

My hand won't spit on itself

*Geometry = Fun
Country Beers = Dumb*

> *Dying With Soft Hands
> A Greater Sin Than Failure*

∧

Says the Poor
White Man

^

Says the Silver Spoon Fuck Whit

The Happier You Are the More
Assholes You Fuck

The Grumpier You Are the More
Assholes You Meet

You take a man's money.
You ride for the
Brand

Shannon Farts in My Mouth

^

Youre going to be okay

Friends don't let friends do shots
together by themselves

Bandera—the cowboy capital
of the world

Eat more Mushrooms
This Bar Still
Sucks

Best BJ in Tulsa
(918)xxx-xxxx
Anytime Day + Night

Bartenders Here Creep.

^

Nah, don't flatter yourself

I puked here 11/19/22

Abortions 4 EVER

Vote   4   Bobby   4   A
Good Time

Become God

Seth Won't Come Here

I See You

*TWO

SITTING ON THE GROUND ANYWHERE

[31] ZERO SUM ZERO VIA NEGATIVE

God.

Samuel Butler: I don't know
what is more childish: to
define God's existence or to
define him.

Here in the Rothko Chapel
at noon, on a Sunday, the
sun this morning came out
earlier after a rainstorm—

and I pray on the ground here
until I have a feeling, something
like Albert Einstein said:

Science without religion is lame.
Science without religion is
blind.

And how to realize God while
driving a car, or typing on a
computer?

And love is found through
loving,

or as Master Eckhart
would say, God is pure
being of no-thing, the void,
emptiness, let go of God
for the sake of God in
order to feel God;

say thank you and remain
silent, and that is enough.

Ralph Waldo Emerson:

He that thinks most says
least; and art hopes to get
close to nature—and
nature, God.

We know this as a feeling in the
Rothko Chapel on the ground,
sitting on the ground
anywhere—sitting on the
ground anywhere, sitting on the
ground anywhere,

we know this as a feeling in the
Rothko Chapel, tomorrow and
earlier sitting on the ground
anywhere, driving, typing, sitting on
the ground anywhere and nowhere

absent of God,

God.

We know this,

(love to all while)

sitting on the ground
anywhere.

                    —12/11/22, Houston, Texas

[32] LONE BOX
—for the poets

In the lobby of the *Mayo Hotel*—
with the rhythms of
di Prima, Jim Harrison, Komunyakaa, Van
Landingham, Eileen Myles, Berryman too— the
34 miles-per-hour winds strike downtown, men
and women struggle to remain vertical getting
in and out of cars, hair and materials wild as
villains, the trees root down life,
and my earlier sideways cigarette by the alley

                    dumpster made Kansas picnics,

        the cardboard boxes shuffling bowling pins
after spares,

as we sought shelter,

                    that lone box sitting still as Buddha.

If you weren't looking you might think
                    the sun and blue sky
                    outside
        or the jazz music inside on velvet couches
                                    was Friday's
metaphysical best rather than Dante's
precursor,

            invisible assault on humanity's footsteps;
the Mayo built in 1910 amid similar American
dust-ups:

            To build an empire takes a scroll
of nameless workmen in windstorms,

            and the music on the pages of lobbies

                    does play on.

                                        —3/31/22

[33] MONDAY AFTERNOON

The black dog named
James Wright swims
through the green yard,
and to my right the dark
            plastic trashcan filled with rainwater
                        feels out of
place next to the

                        cedar tree of
                        feathered emeralds.

        The sunflowers and red poppies to the left
approach union, the sky a movie screen:

And *yes* the generous tree above
                    with white flowers
              on dying branches maintains
a large distinguished
            presence in our yard, like an older
aristocratic bohemian woman over for green tea—

    like Patti Smith
on the back patio.

    She blocks the sun, and I go in
and out of her shadows.

           Very soon there will be apples,
and Lloyd and I will eat them.

The band called *The Band* plays out the boombox.

           We have yet to waste our

                    lives.

    —4/12/20, Corvallis, Oregon

[34] CONTEXT PAPER PART 2, or AUTOBIOGRAPHY
    —for Jim Moore

i've been a ghost for six months

phantom of imagination And i am leading
a quiet life at Shades of Brown here in Red
Dirt Blue Sky Amarillo Afternoon after
Austin Library Houston

Bayou Rockport Beach and Joshua's
Trees Diane's Eggs and
Cole's Cloud Marfa on Halloween
Kiko's Farm i was born in Singapore
and seen the
faces of a thousand lunatics Gone
Medan and Jakarta until the
beaches turned Helicopter New
Zealand boxing Australia Hong
Kong's Soups Amsterdam bicycles
Johannesburg Train Stations
Portugal Expresso Prague Chess
Boards French Soccer Austrian
Opera Irish Parking Lots NYC
Fire Escapes Vermont Trophy
Wives Providence College Students
Dry County Whiskey Seattle
Bridges Indiana Kayaks West
Virginia Boondocks Trinidad
Jet Sets Delhi Landings Fiji
Dreamscapes Montreal Red Lights
Kenyan Bohemia Balinese Women
lions Alabama Drum Circles Mexico
Hallucinations Maine Murders
Harvard Statues Spanish
Requiems California Hotels
30 Days on the Greyhound
Perth Heart Break Panama
Missouri Motels and Swedish
Penthouses i've been there Done that
Seen you Smoked this Forgotten
those And *why not?* PhD National
rankings Public Martyrs Public
hangings Public Readings clubs
committees teams salaries
recommendations of employment

neighborhood building city
breakdown created destroyed built
up let go stayed moved on returned
preferred not to and imagined
otherwise whaddya got Jump here
fill out that say this vote Her double
down and those scrolls
(dis)remember all of it And you
might read that i've fled places jobs
towns women clubs constitutions
ideologies and have stayed and
gotten into too many fights too and
and and sicknesses might even hear
i own it Ayahuasca taught me that
identity doesn't exist i am moving
particles You are moving particles so
best not to write about it just live
IT—those moving particles my
family the world friends The Earth
my experiences YOURS
One Experience the Source of
oceans/minds forgive forget then
remember forgive Love then
Breathe stay go stay go exhale
inhale until the trees are talking
Letters get written to the ether and all
words get distilled into one invisible
embrace my Context Your context
Whitman knew this
marriage divorce Life death
resistance Force one wave of our
Ocean in Shades of Brown and
many shades and lights and open
Spaces sure i've had some
Experiences and done some things but
we all share one Resume one

document of unlocked doors a C.V.
connecting us to those eagles at the
Gathering Place or the Door to the
Mercury Lounge say hello to the Big
Fish

My autobiography Your contexts burn up
                              into infinite

fireworks of blinking lights
and God knows

                    we   are   all
          the Sky canvas
                         and gods know
          we

are   the   skies

     double down   double   on   that
open   wide

                    xo—3/29/23

[35] ALIVE AT THE MERCURY LOUNGE
BLUEGRASS BRUNCH

Played poker last night and lost my ass, sort

of. And at the Mercury Lounge for the Sunday

afternoon Bluegrass Brunch:

The band on stage in overalls and sunglasses

with long hair looks like Lynyrd Skynyrd voted

for Ralph Nader if Ralph Nader shot Ted Nugent
then drank bourbon and kombucha and ate
cheeseburgers after doing hot yoga for a cool
thirty minutes while smoking cigarettes barefoot
on grass; they play their brand of progressive
Southern Rock that could get thousands dancing
at an amphitheater anywhere, but instead a
packed Mercury 138 deep (my count), the small
gem, one of the best music venues in America,
and the best music playing in the state of
Oklahoma at this very moment, and I would bet
all my poker chips on that, and I wouldn't lose
this time.

Tomorrow's Monday and maybe I'll
get my life together.

The sun is in the clear sky again in Tulsa, the
half of the building that shares Dalesandro's
still burned out across the street, and James
Wright had it wrong:

The Mercury is our church right now.

      I am still hurting but I am proud.

The best musicians in Tulsa come here to play

      their souls out every Sunday, and it is

special: pure, unabashed musical freedom,

      and this is my definition of America.

I should know. I'm not a musician, but I've been

      to about 500 live music concerts

in this country in nearly every state, and I know

      a rarity when I see one.

I am going to remember this moment; I am

      going to remember staying in this very
moment, and being in this moment; this is a
juxtaposition and arrangement of cliches in
creative unique ways, which is all writing is,
Ezra Pound was wrong, and this is all new,
this band's creation, all of it, and God bless
you all— the band takes five but really it's
more like 40

(and just remember to read the graffiti writing
on the walls of the men's bathroom),

and I think about all of the people laughing
and smiling and happy and going about their
lives here, as I am in limbo/some weird 'tween
purgatory state

I am trying to learn from and never forget, yet

the good people in this moment do give me hope.

Amy Sue here, the woman I just talked to is
a very good person, and one of the musicians
says:

"There are Girl Scout cookies on the front patio,"

and another guy yells out: "That seems
inappropriate!"

And some old guy with a Brian Wilson haircut
has a t-shirt that says "I am part of the problem,"

and a woman behind me says,
"I am just an addict. I go to Al-Anon,"

and the guy behind her says, "Isn't
that for children and partners of
alcoholics?"

and the woman says, "Yeah, but that's as far as
I've gotten, to complain about other addicts"

and yesterday I felt like dying, but today I think
I'll just listen to music and go for a walk, and as
the band gets back on stage the guy next to me
says,

"Well, I guess that'sa version of a five-minute
break";

he rolls a craps dice game with his girlfriend as
he says this, and I say,

"What's time? Just throw dice" and he

laughs and I laugh, and the band starts up
again, and the crowd is more drunk,

and they play brilliantly like before—the joy and
madness cohere perfectly, the band raises their
glasses to a

TEAM DRINK

—and I do feel like I am in Linklater's
Dazed and Confused or some such movie
and fast forward

a few decades and the kids are now adults and
maybe babysitters or grandparents are at home,
at least neighbors, and they are here for a good
time and music, letting loose for four hours, as
afforded; there are young people here too—who
probably have no idea who Linklater is nor have
seen *Dazed and Confused* and are just dazed and
drunk and dancing and having a good time like
any red-blooded human would and should do,
and obviously have no kids, and the accumulated
band and sounds are fantastic and all is fine in
this moment and the band picks up again and all
is, yes, *fan*—they build up to a crescendo and the
sun is out,

Dalesandro's is still next to a burned-out
building and lovely people are dancing and
Sunday and all of it and yells of joy and
momentary gladness ("forget your week!") and
I just burned a hole in my journal while writing
this but everyone cheers and claps and in this
moment nothing like it, Hank Anderson would
have been proud, I never want this to end, this

is one of the best musical experiences I have ever
had, and I am proud to be here, on this Tulsa
Sunday afternoon for pure music and enjoyment:

we are primed for it, everyone is primed for
             this—the Sunday

Bluegrass Brunch, and the drum solo and all-
             out jam and I

never want to leave, claps all around,
             better than church,

a soulful congregation is what has been created,
             and they deserve it,

the goodness has been purely embraced,
                          and all of the bad

tattoos and mistakes have been forgiven,

             and, yes, James Wright had it wrong:

We have not wasted our lives; beautiful

                          women are dancing,

             Hank Anderson wouldn't have
had it any other way,

on a Sunday afternoon with the music
             and the sky,

and I am hanging in there.

                          —3/5/23

[36] ON BRAND

"Sometimes you gotta try a little harder."
—Melissa Carper

Carl Carbonell on stage playing a sweet song
about Memphis and driving home to Tulsa and
turning 17 and cheap beer and gas— and I think
about my night last night with a former love of
my life. I still love her, but when you haven't
been with a particular person for a dozen years,
you start with liking them, or at least you say
out loud that you do while holding back. Because
my problem, and maybe you have this problem
too, is that once I love someone I love them
forever. Even if they've hit me, spoken poorly
towards me, lied to me, cheated, betrayed me,
etc. I still love them. And I still care about them.
The band has now taken a set break and Sturgill
Simpson plays out of speakers about turtles all
the way down the line— and space and time.
My life has been a series of bad timing, but I'm
trying to change that. I'm trying to change how I
love while trying not to change anything at all.

—5/16/23

[37] AT *LINDA-MAR*

. . . burger place in West Tulsa, I sit in a booth
with Andy Griffith forever on the television. This
is a throwback, Tulsa Speedway memorabilia
included.

Sun going down on this industrial stretch, signs

for Bartlesville and Okmulgee. The Linda-Mar
cheeseburger (with everything) is quite good, a
fine nod &

throwback too. Sometimes I wonder how the fuck
I got here— not to this burger place but to all of
it. This is not Mayberry or even Springfield, and
sometimes I feel like I'm walking

through another man's dream. In his dream he
sees the Quick Trip across the street, Taco Bell on
the corner, and hears the highway sounds as I do,
but in his dream he knows the how

and why questions as well as the answers—and
I have neither questions nor answers, only
observations such as the sun is going down over
West Tulsa or statements such as I don't

know how the fuck I got here. When I see that
man, I'll ask him what his dream means and which
highway I should take to get back to something
green, or at least my own dreamscape.

And later in the night Danno Simpson, a young
musician (hat backwards) out of Ft. Collins,
Colorado, will channel his country vocal belts on
stage as his brilliant brand of

throwback too. He will perform after a wedding
has taken place at the bar, the glowing bride will

stand next to the stage in her dress, *the groom is
around here somewhere*,

floating through that man's dream, hoping for her

version of heaven, or at least a life she can call
her own, a life we all can remember the words to,
maybe even sing along.

—6/15/23

[38] GREY-WHITE CANVAS

The tree beyond the powerlines is shaped like a
brain that shakes and sways rhythmically in the
foreground of a grey-white canvas.

Storm coming, and the singer who channels
Janis Joplin inside offers kaleidoscopic shelter.

In the windowless smoking room, people eat and
congregate around cherry-red cocktails. The
shaggy brown dog's water bowl's empty below
the bench, so he walks inside.

It's the beginning of Friday night, the taco truck
in the parking lot's "open" sign blinks a circle,
and somewhere somehow we will create our own
weather patterns.

The chain-smoking Santa Claus coughs a lung
and I feel for him, his soul a coral reef.

Janis's drummer goes off, cherry red drains,
and the BBQ inside is free for the taking, as is
the rest of the weekend.

It is raining now, tomorrow morning I'll play
tennis, but tonight I'll be open to all of it.

Now at Dalesandro's at the bar, a world away from Mercury, eating fresh bread and drinking barreled scotch.

And later in the night you will tell a woman at another bar that you have no interest in online dating and that you still intentionally have a flip phone. She will tell you that "you haven't evolved" and then she will cry, and you will go home wondering where the hell the night went.

And, by the way, I do think it is okay to like the work of artists whom others consider monsters.

    —5/19/23

[39] MEMORIAL DAY PATIO

Our insides are mysteries to
everyone else—

      the outer layers only a
small percentage: and within
those interior islands, colliding
landscapes and untouched
villages, some of which are waiting
for constellations of meaning,
mythmaking or occasional
understanding, little makes sense
usually—but sometimes

we share ground over bread,
sometimes over biochemical
philosophies or transcendental

handshakes. We strive for
common union, solitary
revelation, notions that
mysteries can be elaborated:

        trying our best to connect

those tapestries and illuminate

neon blueprints and burned-out

skeletons

that guide us,
pretending just long
enough,

lest the lights collide,

for invigoration,

           ghosts too of war heroes' choices.

    —5/29/23

[40] YOU WEREN'T   YOUR MAMA'S ONLY BOY

A poem is a naked person, and I

just saw an independent Italian film

starring Penelope Cruz at the Circle

Cinema. Penelope plays a very good

mother in Rome in the 1970s, and she

radiated off the screen.

At the Whittier Bar in a booth by myself drinking
a Miller High Life 12-ounce can, bad hip hop plays
out of speakers, one dude plays a Halloween pin
ball machine, and the large *SCUM* sign greets
every customer.

Some people want to glorify dive bars or even
someone such as Townes Van Zandt. The truth
is, even though I love him, Townes was from a
wealthy Houston family and didn't have to live
like he did.

Here's one for a song too though:

My mother is down to 90 pounds and is about
to die, my father grieves and wades in a cloud of
intense reclusion, and my parents live in a trailer
in Texas and are so broke that their trailer's a.c.
just went out in the 100-degree heat and they had
to pay for the repair of it on a payment plan.

And I can only pray for their recovery.

The truth is Townes has been glorified by many
people who have felt like slumming it for a while.

But I do love him.

My ex-wife called me in
a hysterical rage earlier,
something about an
address and some boxes

in a garage, and

my mother on the phone
today started crying
because she has lost her
memory and is in so much
pain,

and I'm about to get really drunk
tonight. Tomorrow I'll be hungover and
play tennis like a semi-professional and
pray for my sins and hypocrisy, and
then probably get drunk again.

And in the parking lot of this bar a man is
passed out in his van with all of the doors open.
He just had a seizure and threw up on himself.
I called 9-1-1, there's a pink sunset right now in
Tulsa and an ambulance on its way.

Now at Thelma's Bar the Brad James Band
practices before the crowd comes. I'm the only
one here and the sun has yet to go down. Maybe
Pancho killed Lefty in a knife fight. Maybe they
imagined all of it. Or maybe I'll call my cousin
who is in prison in Texas.

And later that Saturday night there was a
tornado, or at least 100 mph winds, the worst
Tulsa's had in over a decade—and the Brad
James Band played through the rain and
violence to about 20 of us like we were on the
Titanic. My friend John was there after seeing
the Flaming Lips.

John and I braved the weather, got drenched

and wind-turned walking back to the Whittier
Bar, which was without electricity and only
accepting cash. The winds died down a bit after
midnight, so we said *mighttaswell* and decided
to drive through the wreckage, the Corolla
zigzagging around fallen trees and powerlines
(cracking its front bumper on part of a tree in the
street, triaged with duct tape now),

and

> I went to bed soaking wet
> in the garage apartment,
>
> imagining paradise.

The next morning I woke up to apocalyptic debris
and a city-wide power outage. Everyone had
brought out chainsaws to cut the fallen trees
in the streets; no stoplights were working, cars
everywhere on sidewalks, the food in my fridge
was going bad, so I decided to drive to Fayetteville
to see a friend, swim in unnamed rivers, and read
a few e.e. cummings poems under lamplight with
nods towards corner less tomorrows. All is fine

> and *Hi How Are You* . . . best not to
>
> waste your life,

how town,
> best not to waste your life.
>
> *—6/19/23, Fayetteville, Arkansas*

[41] POOL CAPACITY: 33 PERSONS
[*AND A THOUSAND ROADS TO GET
THERE]

At Thurman's Lodge (*pool capacity: 33 persons*)

I'm the only guest. I sit by their small pool
most of the day eating vegetables and fruit and
sandwiches, smoking cigarettes while reading
Joan Didion, Sam Shepard, and the *Bhagavad
Gita*. The kind owner of the lodge gave me a
lesson about the Gita earlier, and last night I
played 8-ball with some friendly locals and did
not lose a game.

There are times in our lives when we
notice the trees more, when we see someone's
eyes. Later today I will go to the Gazebo
Bookshop

(*to speak with Victoria),

the Thorncrown Chapel and maybe
hike a mountain.

Tomorrow Beaver Lake and perhaps a creek for
swimming, a burger at Sparky's, or maybe I'll
sleep in my camping hammock before making
my way back to Fayetteville.

*Because you see:

The world has opened up again, a
return to skylark's choices …

a return

to that heart's gaze of raindown offering,
all a landscape for the Ozark keenness, all a
dreamscape for our light springdom . . .

      . . . and at the Thorncrown—a glass chapel
in the woods on a mountain

           side—I feel God as I open the
Holy Bible to Psalm 150:6,

"Let everything that has breath praise the
         Lord" and think everything not
         everyone,

which means praise comes not only in vocal
articulations but in movements and stillness
and nothingness and actions/energies and
invisibilities, inanimate/animate—thoughts:
and, yes, the construction and life

of a glass chapel in the woods of an Arkansas

mountainside. I breathe as you breathe,
        I am as you are, and we lock

           eyes amid common union of
the eyeless universe of return and dirt
            and return.

* We all know this: Do not waste your time.
Embrace the is and cherish every moment. The
glory is there. We don't need immaculate glass
chapels or architectural marvels in the woods
to remind us of this, nor ayahuasca or Oregon
shamans nor priests or monks after cold plunges
or desert treks or putting myself at the precipice

of the edge, and I certainly don't need cigarettes, et al (as much as all of this is fine & good, and I mean that) because the glory is there, and breathe out. You have arrived. We all have. And my apologies and penance too (tax included but no attorneys needed);

we all have:

Sincerely, with 33 guests and a mountain proud . . .

. . . and after driving the winding Ozarks in the injured Corolla,

I settle on a spot

deep in the woods near the White River and think in my solitary contemplation: I want what

everything wants, love and friendship and intimacy and care and happiness and peace. Most of all peace. And gods grant us the breaths that takes . . .

. . . and later now as I sit on a small wooden bridge over a pond close to the river, I do contemplate further: yes, we all want the same things. Everything wants the same things—

and a thousand roads to get there . . .
and a thousand

roads through that one eyeball and:

you are enough.

. . . as am i . . .

    (As you . . .)

. . . as we . . . God bless and speed and a thousand
miles to get there . . .

    . . . among manifold notes:

      bereft of those mentioned songs . . .
over ridges & rivers . . . towards

the bath of light at moonlit dawn amid rain
thoughts and Rothko and Thorncrown and all of
you
    turned forays into Wild & Blue . . .

    double down those B-sides too, sitting on the
        ground

anywhere . . .

sitting on the ground anywhere. Sitting on the
ground . . . with light in the back of our heads
perfectly screaming for obliteration of all that we
think we know:

the sun's affections & debilitations, the circus
people of any town, or anything else that might
come to—Oregon to Arkansas and a mountain
proud; a vagabond meets a cocktail waitress

    and they go swimming.

    —6/22/23, Eureka Springs, Arkansas

[42] SAID SHARDS OF COSMIC PATCHWORK SCATTERINGS [*thus:]

. . . even if I admit my heart is a crystal soldier,

nothing changes. I don't have to articulate

shattered pieces stuck

with adhesive and duct tape and
willpower or crossed fingers, half

-broken or

semi put-
together—Corolla as metaphor—less of a mess,
enough.

   . . . just say that I have felt and do feel

intensely and am trying my best at forward

motion, for good health and entertainment(s)

of   [   ].
I'll

admit I'm a [

                                             ]

who runs as fast as they can into that stone
wall, knowing pieces will eventually

penetrate, float off into the ether as
                    all of us:

(together, xo: . . . and remember to say
hello to your)

neighbors.

—6/25/23, Fayetteville, Arkansas
*

(***p.s.** Northwest Arkansas, thanks to you as
well.)
*

[43] TOMORROW WE WILL GO TO BRUNCH

At the Saturn Room—Tulsa's best tiki bar.

> Imagine Fiji
> and Oklahoma having a baby,
> and the baby has a rainbow of
> lit-up balls.

$6 shot and beer.

> Three young women bartend as
> sympatico.

Sympatica?

> They take a break in unison to smoke
> cannabis in the alleyway behind the bar.

Bob Marley plays out speakers then
Urge Overkill. Uma Thurman

> would agree with this place.

After smoking a cigarette outside
and going back inside, even
though no one is tending bar, I
have a free shot of tequila upon
return to this journal.

Sun going down:

Plastic flowers and velvet paintings
complement the long carved wooden

> bar made from a tree on
> an island in the Pacific,

> or Catoosa,

and I just got word an old
friend will be driving here
tonight:

> The joy of Saturday, the
> joy of okay Fiji, and the
> miracles of your lives.

I have never owned the

night, but I did buy it once in

Providence, Rhode Island,

> on layaway:

> 36 installments of love
> after dancing
> through

countless carnivals in OKC, Greenpoint/the
Lower East Side, Austin/Georgetown and Real de
Catorce:

> those proven possibilities and
> lasting gratitude for showing
> me how to love when I was a

                              younger man— and for

being who you are. Thank you for reminding

me I should continue. You are beautiful,
a good one, and you deserve to get back

to

        your blossoms too. God speed for that,
lady, the best will come, dancing to steel guitar
barefoot in a patch of

            grass—& cheers to okay tiki Fiji too:

        Winslow and the rest of us await said
screaming light.

                        −7/1/23

[44] TULSA NON-POEM
                —*for SMC*

"Love is the only God that I'll ever believe in."
        —Woody Guthrie

Alone in the backyard of this *South Cincinnati
Avenue garage apartment,*

I see the possibilities of sunset's musings.

My life is not a reality show
but I do write about reality.

Classical music softly plays out of a small
radio, three books of poems from

the *Tulsa Downtown Public Library*, a *Joy
to the World* coffee mug given to me by a dear
person who is braving disease; a 40-year-old
oak tree in front of me, three red chairs (two
waiting for friends), and a peaceful guess that
my life is about to change.

And now at the Tam Bao Buddhist Temple,
I know all will be okay regardless of what
happens. Sundays happen for a reason, yet only
if you believe in reasons—which I do now. There
is serenity here even though I can still hear
the traffic noises. The largest Buddha statue
in Oklahoma in front of me, 72 degrees this
morning, birds are chirping and the breeze takes
my mind to clouds on left, blue sky right:

a hawk takes his time floating
around a tree beyond.

A pond waves in the distance, so I walk— and
on the bridge of that pond, I see and hear ducks
that drown the traffic noise, and I am reminded:
The motions of our lives have led us to this very
moment, and I can say with certainty that I
know what I'm doing for the first time in a long
while— with all of my beating heart, my bleeding
being and the misguided dream of the poetic
language of my youth. Yet older now with scars
and memories disguised as flowers, prayers,
and a landscape—of red dirt and gratitude, that
collateral music in physical reality.

And the largest Buddha statue
in Oklahoma in front of me

kills my ego.

Christianity and capitalism don't
work well together,
as the material tries to destroy
the spiritual.

We don't know why humanity
is here.

Thanks for reading.

What have we done to the planet?
What have we done to each other?

Most of my adult life has been
a country song with women and
whiskey and so on,

but I don't write country songs
anymore.

And after listening to a Drive-
Bye Truckers live album in the
Corolla, and after speaking with
my sweet parents on the telephone—
whom I love and am grateful for
what they've done for me—
I find myself in front of the
tombstone of Claude Russell Bridges,
Sir Leon Russell, the Master
Of Space & Time himself,
player of that wizard piano.

And let us not forget that
Adolf Hitler declared himself
a Catholic.
Use your knives only to make
sandwiches.

Put down your knives and
just make sandwiches.

It has been a pleasant day
with mushrooms
and all of you.

For I have survived and thank you all for the
non-poems. Sincerely (again) as the clearly
broken words we swear by. David Shields was
right:

Our lives are a collage, written in graffiti on the
bathroom walls of the Mercury Lounge—

HIPPIES PARK IN BACK

                                                    yet
              everybody's welcome.

[p.s.] ROYALTY IN EXILE

*Looking for the answers in all the same things,
I turned my life into another man's dream.
Locked up and cold, feeling bitter and old,
say that everything happens for a reason.
What's the point when there's no point at all?*

What's the reason behind this mess,
or do we get to make that call?
Is there anybody out there to help me
understand?
Trying to find my way to be a better man.

You were growing tired of holding things down.
How could you keep us together when I'm never
around?
Nights grew long, days flew by,
I thought I could keep you satisfied.
What's the point when there's no point at all?
What's the reason behind this mess,
or do we get to make that call?
Is there anybody out there to help me
understand?
Trying to find my way to be a better man.

> **You've been working hard,**
> **and I've been playing in bars.**
> **I guess it's fair to say it ain't fair at all.**
> **Should've seen the closing signs.**
> *You were always on my mind.*
> **I think it's safe to say we know how this**
> **one ends.**

What's the point when there's no point at all?
What's the reason behind this mess,
or do we get to make that call?
Is there anybody out there to help me
understand?
Trying to find my way, trying to find my way,
trying to find my way to be a better man—
a better man. Oh, a better man.

Better man.

Royalty In Exile?

S.E. Hinton wrote about this condition in relation
to the Motor-cycle Boy in **Rumble Fish**, a
superior
book and movie to *The Outsiders*, and I think it
means a person has been born into the
wrong time and/or place yet it's so obvious
they are rare and that with one slight tilt of the
world's axis they would have gotten their proper
due.

I've felt this when I've seen Chris Blevins
perform,
but I also feel it every time I see Paul Benjaman
play the guitar.

His stage commentary 'tween songs tonight:

"Called beat the heat, or otherwise called
a brain freeze. Stunned either way."

But royalty in exile

R.I.E?

*Answer: A presence
that feels otherworldly,
or between—both
worlds and ideas.

Bad timing,

essentially,

or maybe the rest of us have not caught up

(and, by the way,
this is not unrelated to the definition of **ether:**

> *a pleasant-smelling colorless volatile
> liquid that is highly flammable.*

> **OR:** *the clear sky;* **the upper regions
> of air beyond the clouds.**

> **OR:** *air regarded as a medium for radio.*

> **OR:** *a very* **rarefied and highly
> elastic substance** *formerly believed
> to permeate all space, including the*
> **interstices between the particles of
> matter,** *and to be the medium whose
> vibrations constituted light and other
> electromagnetic radiation.*

; anyway, Paul Benjaman does seem to be
channeling
                    transcendence tonight)

In a way he plays for himself and we
are just fortunate enough to be
witnessing it—and on some level
everyone knows this: that is, if they
are paying attention.

                    That's the royalty part—the

exile part either means he is in the
wrong city or is too good for this world.

      I believe the latter but hope for the former
      because I want to think more highly
      of the world:

"Yeah, hanging out at Merc,
having a good time once again.
I will mention that it's Zach's
birthday back here on the
drums. Been working on this
song for him all week, ha."

Paul Benjaman: a combination of
Waylon Jennings, Ronnie Van
Zandt, Burnside(s) and throw in
the name of a skilled

                blues

guitarist you've never heard of
too. The sound: good-
special-real and yes . . .

            royal.

*Royal: That's the word,

which translates as purgatory,
'tween category of people who are
too good (for whatever reasons).

It reminds me of the book

The Crying of Lot 49:

the connections are specious and nothing
logically adds up because the timing is off,

        but we all
        know the quality
        is there because
        what's in front is

            such an

obvious truth
and the unlikely combinations do make
good sense.

I will call Paul Benjaman The
Truth. His guitar shouts it. It and he
are not Paul Pierce, but they (he and his guitar)
comprise the truth:

The Tulsa Truth.

        We all are better off for being here:
        in our brilliant anonymity.

And the world knows that every human
being has their moment. It just depends if
the right people notice (yet there are no
right people, we know this too),

        or if anyone notices at all—

doesn't matter though.

We all know it. When we see/hear it, usually.
It does depend on if you are paying attention.

And I'll admit what I've done recently
could be perceived as insanity: leaving
a beautiful-successful-wealthy woman,

Oregon,

a cushy life, a 400K house and all of the
comforts in the world, giving up my side
of the house and the bank account, taking
a few grand for another roadtrip across

America and to *check in* on Texas—

now Tulsa, living modestly, barely
getting by as a humble Buddhist poet
and occasional tennis teaching pro.
And about to start teaching writing
and literature again after this
stripped-down year of self-imposed
contemplative sabbatical.

I would have it no other way. I've made
what I consider the right decision(s).
I didn't love her and I was miserable (and
she cheated on me and lied about it
anyway, though I do still think she is a good
person, even though she lost her soul to the
technocracy and her mother is a
monster and never taught her how to truly love,

which maybe is neither here nor there,
and in a way I do still love her but not
in a way that makes sense for marriage. So I
took this year to contemplate and ask for for-
giveness and find a better way. God knows

I made a lot of mistakes too, but what I now
more softly and clearly better realize is that
in the approach of mind-body-spirit that
intimacy of *spirit* is most important and true,
and that this applies most prominently to any
relationship, romantic or otherwise, and that
now is finally the appropriate time to move on
with my life in more positive and enriching ways,
yet I will not, not ever, never, forget this past year.

> **For, to love is to feel pain and there
> ain't no way around it,**

said a smart man once.

I do wake up every day with the attempt to
be a better man. I sincerely do, and I
wish all the best and good fortune
for her as well).

I guess in a way I'm royalty in exile at times
too, but, regardless, it is time for all of us
to live our lives, and we can thank the likes
of the Paul Benjamans and S.E. Hintons and
Lance Roarks and Melissa Carpers

    and Burnsides

of this world for that.

> *They remind
> us of the lessons*
> **written in graffiti
> on the moon.**

You just have to look up every once in a while

and read the obvious writings illuminated
by that natural light.

And after the show, I spoke with Paul's
lady friend and Paul, and they are both
sweet people. Their romance screams kind-
ness. His lady friend agrees that Paul is
royalty in exile and explains that he is an even
better man than guitar player, and I do believe
that. He talked about giving back to the younger
Tulsa musicians because the older musicians
did the same for him when he was coming up,
and it occurs to me more aptly that the
musicians
of this town are

collectively
representative

of royalty in exile.

Hinton knew this about certain people and her
town,

and you and I

can still witness it among the Tulsa Sound today.

Just remember to read the graffiti on the
moon

every once in a while
(or at least the detritus on the sides of
buildings
and/or on bathrooms walls):

to throw a few dollars
in the various buckets,

and to say
　　　please
and thank you.

(*And remember
　　to say hello
　　　　to your
　　　　　neighbors.)

—July 13, 2023

[p.p.s.] AND THIS IS ALSO A POEM, YOUNG MAN
—for whom it may concern

Trust your gut and your instincts.
Don't apologize if you've done nothing wrong.

But apologize anyway.

Trust your heart.
If something feels like madness it probably is.
Don't be afraid to leave a bad situation.

But do kindly fight

For what you think is right.
Don't hesitate to point out what is good

And to deeply appreciate it.

Don't be afraid to apologize when you are wrong
yet

Don't stay in something for the wrong reasons

Because other people expect you to.

People are not afterthoughts

Nor is your life.

Remain true to yourself
And remember your ideals and principles.
Remember your morals.

Think, say, and do what you know is right.

Cherish every human being
And realize that every child has a chance.

See past uniforms and masks.

Get off your screens
Go outside

And love with all you've got

In physical reality.

Keep reading.
Keep learning.
Learn how to hunt
And fish how to
Perform calculus and
Write beautifully
Master tennis
Remember good
Music and that
Sunflowers are
More Important
Than books.

Make mistakes
Learn from them

And feel good

About it.

Learn to live on your own.

To exist on your own.

Remember to say hello
To your neighbors

And to say I love you

Every chance you get.

The patriarchy sucks
But so does the matriarchy.
All isms are questionable
And all groups are susceptible
To cruelty and Injustice

Yet remember that any mob

Has the potential for
Virtue.

All human beings are
Fallible.

Be a part of
The world

But not of it.

Do and do not

Join

All groups.

Exist
As
Moving

Particles as
Solid and
Ether.

Question everything.

Question nothing.

Apologize anyway.

Show gratitude.

Count your blessings.

Pay attention.

Speak up

But remain quiet.

Kindness trumps everything but do not let people
take advantage.

You know what to do: love, compassion,

Empathy, kindness, tenderness, patience,
Impermanence,

Openness, understanding, forgiveness, Humility,
humanity, repeat . . .

This is a poem.

And, yes, there is a lot left.
You have a lot left.

This is a poem about something:

Do not worry about cliches
or fads.

All dogs and horses

Are superior.

The earth is greater

Than humans.

Create.

We are all connected.

Everything is connected.

Double down.

Double:

On that open wide

And

Forgive

Forget

And

Forgive.

Love again.

Give. Do what You feel is

Truly best.

Go where you feel is truly best.

Love who you feel is truly best.

Love the worst as well.

Forgive.

Stay still.
Sit on the ground.

Believe it

But don't fool yourself.

And remember
That the world
Is changing
For better and worse

And

Or not changing
At all

And that you can be a poet

And a good person
A better person
Even with a 100-word vocabulary.

No Bullshit.

Then:

You will not have wasted your life.

Om
Ah
Peace.
Mani
Padme hum.

Repeat.

And remember to love
Get your heart obliterated

Get up

Then love again.

Repeat.

Repeat.

And repeat.

—July 18, 2023

VERY SHORT BIO

this is walter moore's third book with emp
books. sometimes he naps.

REALLY LONG BIO

Dr. Walter Moore or Walt was born in Singapore, has been to 40 countries and 47 U.S. states and has lived in about twenty cities and towns around the world: from Jakarta, Indonesia; Houston and Austin, Texas; Denver, Colorado; Oklahoma City; Brooklyn, New York, and Carmel, California, to Providence, Rhode Island; Seattle, Washington, and Perth, Australia, among other places.

Dr. Moore has taught 147 lower and upper-level college courses in English, academic writing, creative writing, literature, American Studies, and film in places as varied as Southwestern University, Mercer County Community College, the University of Rhode Island, and the University of Washington Tacoma. He's won exactly eleven teaching awards. 2021-2022 marked his fifth year of teaching at Oregon State University and his twentieth year of teaching at the college level overall. He holds a BA in English from DePauw University, an MFA in Creative Writing from Texas State University, and a Ph.D. in American Studies from Purdue University (Primary Focus: U.S. Literature; Secondary Foci: Film, Sociology, and Urban Anthropology).

In a former life, he worked as a lifeguard, retail clerk, movie theater usher, lawn guy, line cook, restaurant busboy/ barback/ server, academic tutor, law clerk (he went to law school at Indiana University for one year and four days), and tennis teaching professional (he was a highly ranked junior tennis player, ranked as high as #7 in Colorado and #2 in Oklahoma, and played college tennis at DePauw University where he was First Team ICAC All-Conference two years in a row. He also competed in one season of college club soccer in Australia).

More recently, he's written reading passages for an education textbook company, worked as a journalist for a few newspapers (*San Marcos Daily Herald*, *Williamson County Sun*, etc.), and published poems and stories in various journals (*Experimental Poetry*, *Midwest Review*, etc.). His book of poems *My Lungs Are a Dive Bar*, a series of deadpan / gritty/neo-beat/punkish poems about rural Indiana and urban Washington (some Texas, too) was published by EMP Books in March of 2019. His first novel, *The Phalanx of Houston* (a coming-of-age story about a 26-year-old drifter-bartender with a G.E.D. who returns to his hometown of Houston, Texas, to solve a professional soccer player's murder with his alcoholic father) was released by EMP Books in April of 2021.

His scholarly research interests include 20th-Century American Literature, Film & Culture. His Ph.D. dissertation titled *This is Not a Dissertation*: (Neo)Neo-Bohemian Connections (2015) focuses on how selected literary and cinematic texts speak to the narratives of neo-bohemian gentrification in U.S. cities.

In the summer of 2019, Walt and his LA-based writing partner, Eli Green, sold a film screenplay called *Cut*, a story about bias, despair and redemption in urban law enforcement.

Over the years, Moore has worked as an actor on the stage and on television, having performed in leading and supporting roles in various local stage productions in Austin, Texas; Monterey, California; New York City; and Tacoma, Washington. His big claims to fame include playing a campus hippie in an MTV commercial and a deadbeat roommate in a TV pilot episode of the sitcom *Sisters* for the Oxygen Channel.

Moore has coached several tennis teams (all with winning records, including a few district, regional and conference championships), having served as the Assistant Women's Tennis Coach at Texas State University, Assistant Men's Coach at Southwestern University (TX), Head Girls High School Tennis Coach of the Casady School (OK), Assistant Boys Tennis Coach of Central Catholic High School (IN), and Head Boys' Tennis Coach at Crescent Valley High School (OR). A U.S.P.T.A.-certified professional, he's taught tennis at camps, tennis clubs, country clubs, and resorts (most notably the Topnotch Resort in Stowe, Vermont, which was at the time ranked the #2 tennis resort in the world).

His favorite musician is Patterson Hood; second favorite musician: Steve Earle; favorite movie: *Paris, Texas*; second favorite movie: *Stalker* (*the 1979 Russian version); TV series: *Mad Men*; poet: Walt Whitman; novel: *Sometimes a Great Notion* (by Ken Kesey); and food: breakfast tacos (potato, egg, & cheese with sausage sometimes).

Alongside reading/writing/teaching/acting/coaching, his other joys include playing soccer and tennis, watching movies, bowling, playing pool and table tennis, meditating, hiking, seeing live music, doing nothing in bathrobes, napping, taking cold plunges, soaking in hot tubs or hot springs, and generally hanging out with whomever is around. He is 46 years old but sometimes feels like he's 80, which is why he naps.

He is on a perpetual roadtrip (at least in his mind).

An Addendum of Praise for
Walter Moore's **tulsa non-poems**

"Walter Moore doesn't write poems—he writes portals. To read his latest is to encounter the raw and rough-hewn emotion of midlife upheavals, the startling transcendence of humor and suffering in a Texan's Oklahoma, the atmospheric glow that can emanate from the right dive-bar music9—and so much more. Read these pages for the same reason you would make friends with an alluring stranger: to share this short, messy beautiful life with someone who might just understand."
—John Larison, author of *Whiskey When We're Dry*

"These (non-)poems are clear-eyed and big-hearted—they show you Tulsa from the eyes of a man who's been knocked down but is getting back on his feet. It's all here: bad relationships, good music, Christ at Best Buy, tiki bars, Toyota Corollas, and the most honest graduation speech I've ever read. Like the man says, read if you feel like it. You might learn something."
—Justin St. Germain, author of *Son of a Gun*